Dedicated to my father & mother

THANK YOU

PRINTED IN THE UNITED STATES OF AMERICA

To the Naysayers: Open your mind and learn to unlearn.

Mikazuki Jujitsu Manual; Learn Jujitsu
ISBN 978-0-615-47311-6
Library of Congress Control Number: 2011926823
Copyright© 2011 by Mikazuki Publishing House
Publisher: Mikazuki Publishing House

Illustrations: Hoornaz Mostofizadeh
Foreword by: Amir Tarighat

WARNING! DO NOT PRACTICE THESE TECHNIQUES WITHOUT THE SUPERVISION OF A PROFESSIONAL MARTIAL ARTIST

CONTENTS

Foreword 4

Introduction 5

What is Jujitsu? 6

Ki Development 17

Mikazuki Guard 20

Safety First 22

Breakfalling Techniques 24

Standing Techniques 25

Throws 35

Ground Techniques 42

Self Defense/Escape Techniques 62

Punching 64

Blocking 66

Kicking 68

Gripping/Seizing 72

Attack & Mental Strategies 74

8 Directions of Off Balancing 75

Taking the Initiative 80

Scoring System 82

Kata & Randori 83

Fighting Methods 85

Sparring Tips 86

Understanding Range 87

Understanding Timing 89

5 Grappling Tips 90

How to Defeat a Boxer 92

How to Defeat a Wrestler 94

How to Defeat a Mixed Martial Artist 95

How to Defeat a Karateka 96

How to Fight Multiple Attackers 97

Important Jujitsu Schools 99

Is Jujitsu Japanese in Origin? 100

Jujitsu and the Law 110

Verbal Jujitsu 112

Jujitsu Glossary 115

Counting (Japanese) 120

Jujitsu Tournament Directory 121

References 122

Jujitsu Official Haiku 124

The Final Word 125

FOREWORD

"It is a principle of the art of war that one should simply lay down his life and strike. If one's opponent also does the same, it is an even match. Defeating one's opponent is then a matter of faith and destiny." Yamamoto Tsunetomo, from the Hagakure

The origins of Jujitsu can be traced back to 17th century martial artists in Japan's samurai class. In spite of its widely disputed heritage, experts speculate that the techniques were first employed as a method for fighting armored opponents. Since striking an opponent wearing armor would have been ineffective, they focused on creating a system that would use the opponent's momentum against him. Today, modern Jujitsu practitioners have supplemented and expanded the art.

Kambiz Mostofizadeh's Jujitsu Manual represents his interpretation and development of this ancient martial art form. The Manual serves as an unabridged rendition of Jujitsu, based on his personal experience and innovation, while staying true to the traditional principles of this form. This is evident in the emphasis in bowing, the traditional gi, and the terminology. Throughout the Manual, Kambiz's passion for the art form comes to light and emerges into the narrative that is Jujitsu.

-Amir Tarighat

Introduction

As a individual that has trained in martial arts for the majority of my life, I felt that a manual that best explained the style that I teach and practice would be available to myself, my students, and to other students of the martial arts as a reference. This book will teach you the principles and give you more knowledge about modern jujitsu as it's practiced by Jujitsu. It will not make you a black belt, give you higher ranking, or make you a jujitsu master. Reading a book to become a jujitsu master is like reading a driving manual and "instantly" becoming a driver or reading a medical textbook and then doing heart surgery. You can, however, read a medical textbook and perform heart surgery, but please, first wish your patient and yourself good luck! Please have fun reading my work & enjoy!

What is Jujitsu?

Jujitsu is a martial art that was used by Samurai during their most erratic period of internal political strife, the 15th to 16th century AD. Modern jujitsu is referred to as Gendai jujutsu or modern self defense jujitsu because the style was formed after 1900. Modern jujitsu styles are also known as Goshin Jujitsu. Jujitsu adapted low kicking techniques from karate, throws from judo, and pugilistic techniques used in boxing. Jujitsu applies traditional Japanese philosophies and mannerisms such as bowing. Its training techniques are modern. Jujitsu practitioners train using athletic shoes with their jujutsu gi. Free fighting is done on hardwood floors but throwing and ground grappling is conducted on ¾ inch to 1 inch thick interlocking mats designed for preventing injuries from falls.

Jujitsu stresses the simplification of the application of techniques, streamlining of the training and methods and adaptation of effective techniques from other combative systems. The basis of the Jujitsu defensive posture is it's many "guards", used for the purpose of achieving complete protection against hooks and kicks. Offensively, Jujitsu practitioners use strike or submission attempts in combinations. Circular body movements are used when off balancing, throwing, joint locking and evading. "Jujitsu" literally means yielding techniques.

Jujitsu uses the principle of yielding as the basis for its fighting style. The style emphasizes blending your energy with that of the opponent in order to stop their attack. An example of this would be you entering to clinch your opponent as they strike and off balancing them.

Jujitsu uses punching, kicking, blocking, evasions, seizing, clinching, locking, throwing, tripping, sweeping, defensive escapes , ground fighting , Kata(forms) and Ki development. The system depends on the use of effective techniques, rather than serving other purposes. The rotation of the Jujitsu practicioner is philosophical as well as functional. The rotation and the force that is generated by the rotation, entangles the opponent in the movement and force of your body's rotation. This has the result of making you a moving target which creates visual targeting difficulties for your opponent as he/she attempts a technique. The maneuvering creates effective evasions and makes it much easier for the jujitsu practicioner to avoid attacks. The rotation evades these attacks by maneuvering. Jujitsu is a

goju style or hard/soft style. "Go" means hard in Japanese and "Ju" meaning soft or yielding. The hardness of the Jujitsu style is associated with striking techniques using punches, kicks, and knees. The softness of the style is associated with off balancing, throwing, joint locking, choking or strangling, escapes, evasions, and use of meditation.

The phrase **Ju Yoku Sei Go** translates as **Softness Controls Hardness**. Softness controls hardness because the most resilient things in nature are those that are supple, flexible, adaptable, and able to blend with their environment. Mikazuki Jujitsu's techniques use hard techniques as well but the correct and effective application of techniques is the defining factor. The chances are real that there are people who may be taller than you, stronger than you, faster than you, more intelligent than you, harder punching or kicking than you, or a better grappler. This is precisely the reason the Jujitsu practicioner relies on the principles that guide the style. The use of strikes, off balancing, throws, and submissions in combination is the first principle. The second principle is constant circling which means to not stop maneuvering and moving against your opponent. The loss of maneuvering creates a stationary target that makes it easy for your opponent to be able to attack you. The third principle is the effective use of counter-striking which means that you should actively seek openings or gaps in the defenses of the opponent. If the opponent steps into your kicking range and their left leg was the first part of their body to enter your kicking range, it would be a wasted opportunity for you to not attempt a low roundhouse kick. When your opponent attacks, vulnerabilities are created in their defenses because no individual is able to attack and defend all areas of their body simultaneously.   99.9 percent of martial artists are unable to attack and defend simultaneously. Jujitsu students learn to attack and defend without revealing major gaps by utilizing the Mikazuki Guard.

Yielding's strength can be attested to by the geography of the earth which has been shaped by the vast oceans which inhabit our planet. Water is supple, soft, and flexible.   It takes the shape and form of the item it is contained by, thus it is adaptable. The Jujitsu practicioner must also be adaptable to the opponent, adaptable to harsh training conditions, as well as being adaptable to life's series of positive and negative events.

Building your muscular physique through body

building and weightlifting is good but mentally
and physically becoming accustomed to depending
on your muscles for self defense is not partially
realistic because there may be someone else who
has bigger muscles than you do. By yielding and re-
directing the aggression of that attacker, the jujitsu
practitioner aims to defeat the opponent using their
strength against them.   The use of Shime-Waza or
choking/strangling and Kansetsu-Waza or joint
locking techniques techniques are the main weapons
of submission attack used against an attacker.

When Kansetsu-Waza or Joint Locking
techniques are used, the Jujitsu practitioner
positions themselves so that their body weight is
directed at one part of the opponent's body. For
example, in a shoulder lock, the practitioner is
positioned with their body weight applying pressure to

the shoulder.

If the attacker pushes, the **Jujitsu** defender pulls and redirects. When the attacker pulls, the **jujitsu** defender pushes, thus adding energy to the opponent's attack. Jujitsu allows the weaker individual to defend by using **leverage** and applied technique rather than reliance on strength.

The essence of Jujitsu is adaptability to unknown outcomes. Adaptability on the tatami or training mat, adaptability to life's harsh and sometimes brutal outcomes, and adaptability to your opponent in life and death situations are all part of the way.

The strength of a martial artist emanates from being able to "weather the storm" or survive whatever "card they have been dealt".

According to jujitsu lore, the way that a willow

tree survives a storm by bending before the wind and then whipping back unharmed afterwards, whereas the more rigid cherry tree is easily battered to pieces, demonstrates the strength of yielding.

Principles of Jujitsu

- **Seiryoku Zenyo** (Maximum gain through minimum effort)

  Over time, the principle of ju or yielding or softness in many Jujitsu, Judo and Judo offshoots evolved in to the reliance on strength. Jigoro Kano, who adopted the principle from Jujitsu, believed that incorrect postures, incorrect movements, and attempting to throw before off balancing represented the use and reliance on strength. For the principle of ju to be applied, technical efficiency had to triumph over strength. Using strength to execute a technique is not implementing or utilizing the principle of yielding.

- **Sen** (Taking the Initiative)

Sen or taking the initiative is a principle which states that problems must be dealt with before they arise. In single combat, an opponent's moves should be foreseen and prevented before they arise and at the time they arise.

- **Ju Yoku Sei Go** (Softness Controls Hardness)

Softness controls hardness because the Jujitsu practicioner absorbs and blends with the attacks. This is the meaning of yielding defeats aggression.

Three Virtues of Jujitsu

The monk pursues courage with the warrior as his model and the warrior pursues compassion with the monk as his model **(1).**

The purpose of the 3 virtues is to develop character and instill the following virtues in the practitioner:

- **Courage** – Courage is the most important of the virtues. To have no fear and to act with full awareness, to stand up for right and disavow the wrong is the meaning of courage.
- **Compassion**- To feel the feelings of others and to adjust your temperament based on their feelings.

- **Respect**- To always have respect for yourself, elders, and everyone you come in contact with under all circumstances

氣 Ki Development

Ki means internal energy that resonates and travels within all human bodies. The practice of meditation, breathing, and increasing blood circulation through exercise has been known to increase the level of Ki. The key is to breathe deep and high in your chest, and during the next inhalation/exhalation, breathe from the lower stomach area.

Ki Training

Meditation is used to increase the flow of blood in the body and to stimulate alpha brain waves which in turn create a sense of serenity whilst keeping the individual aware. The increased blood flow in the body also generates greater amounts of oxygen, "theoretically" giving the individual a longer life span. Ki is believed to be the internal energy that runs throughout our bodies and by focusing this internal energy we are able to achieve greater than average actions. A real life example of this could be a mother lifting the side of a car 200 times her own weight when her child was stuck under the car in an accident. Was this mother superhuman or an individual that for a very short period of time was able to focus their internal energy?

Mokuso

Mikazuki Guard

Invincibility is a matter of self-defense;

vulnerability is simply a matter of having gaps.

– WANG XI, ART OF WAR (15)

The Mikazuki Guard is a defensive guard, distinctive to Jujitsu that its practitioners use in free fighting. In contrast to boxing's defensive guards which are designed to stop jabs, reverse punches and uppercuts, the Mikazuki Guard is used to block hooks, jabs, and reverse punches. The right fist is clenched, placed below the left elbow; the left fist is clenched placed on top of the right elbow, with both arms raised to eye level forming a square as a defense. The left forearm is then raised 1 inch to allow for vision. The Mikazuki Guard provides maximum protection for the jujitsuka's ears, eyes, and other vital points while being able to defend and strike or enter for a throw. The Mikazuki Guard does not change when stances are switched. The only punching technique which the Mikazuki Guard is vulnerable to is the uppercut. Techniques which rely on simplicity and leverage are favored, while techniques depending on strength rather than leverage are not.

Jujitsu students learn all aspects of the principles, applications, and development of martial arts by constantly studying and training.

Main Methods

- ❖ **Kuzushi-no-Happo** – Off Balancing Techniques
- ❖ **Nage-Waza** – Throwing techniques
- ❖ **Shime-Waza** – Choking Techniques
- ❖ **Kansetsu-Waza** – Joint Locking Techniques
- ❖ **Ne-Waza** – Ground Grappling Techniques

Safety First

The Jujitsu practicioner should wear a clean, white single weave cotton gi or uniform, tied with a belt, only bearing the patches of Mikazuki Jujitsu. He/she should be wearing running, training or exercise shoes but the shoes should not have protrusions or rugged or sharp points at the bottom of the shoes that can be dangerous to the training partner when sparring. The Jujitsu practicioner should be wearing padded grappling gloves.

There is no striking above the shoulders intentionally or unintentionally when sparring as to maintain the "sport's" quality and prevent injuries. If you are feeling overly tired, out of breath, etc., ask your instructor for a minute break. If you are injured, do not train while you are injured as this could worsen your injury. Wait until you have healed and then start training again.

Careful attention should be paid to maintain complete awareness in order to preserve precise control of your body in respect to the proper application of the technique you are applying.

If you are practicing kicking, then you should occasionally ask your partner if your kicks are too hard or too soft. It is not only very important because of safety reasons, but also this information allows you to practice greater control of your leg that is striking, to be able to kick full speed while delivering ¼ strength, ½ strength, ¾ strength, etc.

Breakfalling Techniques (UKEMI)

Ukemi-Waza

Falling properly and safely is fundamentally important to throwing. The body should curl up and both arms if possible should assist in breaking the fall. Whether the individuals fall back, forward, or on their side, they should break their fall by slapping the ground with the inside of their forearm and their open hand. You should **never** attempt to break your fall by using the palms of your hands and wrists because they will break under your weight.

Standing Techniques

❖ **Kata-Gaeshi**- Shoulder Lock **(Yellow Belt)**

KATA-GAESHI

The Kata-Gaeshi or Twisting Shoulder Lock is a signature Jujitsu technique designed to control . The opponent can be forced to submit, attacked with knee strikes and punches, pushed

off balance, and thrown.

❖ **Kote-Gaeshi** (Wrist Lock) **(Yellow Belt)**

The Kote-Gaeshi or Twisting Wrist Lock torques

the opponent's wrist causing them to submit

from pain or flip their entire body over their wrist.

❖ **Ude-Garami** (Kimura) **(Orange Belt)**

Also called Kimura. Named after Masahiko

Kimura after Kimura defeated Helio Gracie,

ultimately dislocating Gracie's shoulder

through the repeated use of this technique.

❖ **Ude-Gatame** (Pressing Armlock)
 (Orange Belt)

The Ude-Gatame is similar to the Kata-Gaeshi

with this difference that Ude-Gatame

leverages your weight against the opponent's

elbow rather than the opponent's shoulder.

❖ **Ude-Guruma-Jime** (Forearm Winding Choke)
(Orange Belt)

In Ude-Guruma-Jime or Forearm Winding Choke,

your right hand grabs the right collar of your

opponent (your left) and then you close the gap

between your opponent and yourself, causing

your elbow of the hand (which is holding the

collar) to rest on his left shoulder (your right).

Your left arm then reaches around the back of the

opponent and your left hand grips the inside of

your right elbow. The lock around the neck is

tightened by turning both fists slowly in your

direction (without moving your arms).

❖ **Ude-Osae** (Arm Pin) **(Blue Belt)**

As you are standing in left Zenkutsu Datchi or left

front stance, you pivot and move away from the

opponent's reverse punch, then step in and grab the

opponent's punching arm with both hands. Your right pulls the arm across your chest while your left arm pushes away on the opponent's chest. The feeling of having his/her arm pulled in the opposition direction of the body is not only painful but suited for times when punching and kicking an attacker is not warranted.

Ude-Osae

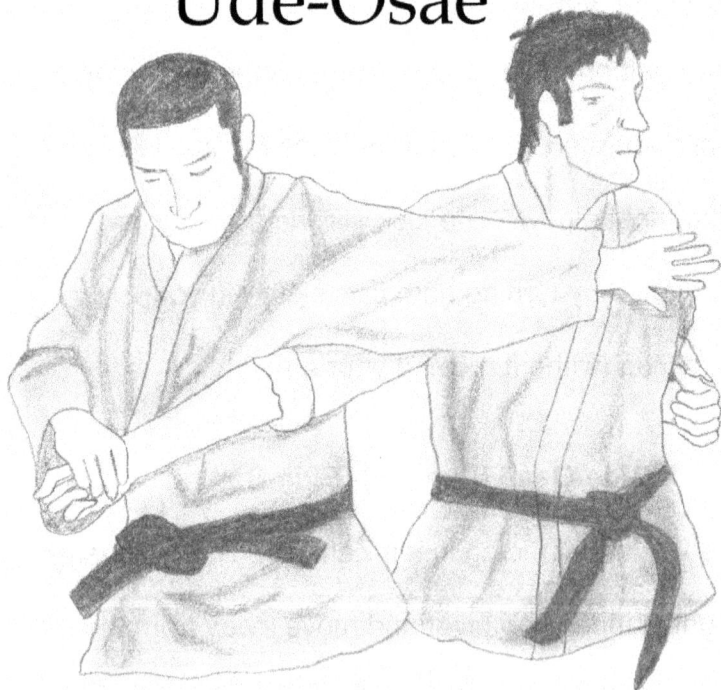

❖ **Jime-Barai** (Step In Choke Sweep)
(Blue Belt)

As you are standing in Zenkutsu Datchi or front stance, you pivot and move away from the opponents punch or kick, you parry the opponent's strike with your jab hand and then step in and wrap your reverse punch hand around the neck of the opponent as in a naked rear choke. Then you turn 180 degrees in the direction of your lead hand causing the "sweep" and your opponent to completely lose balance and fall while you are holding their neck.

❖ Hiji-Gaeshi (Arm Circle Lock) (Green Belt)

Hiji-Gaeshi

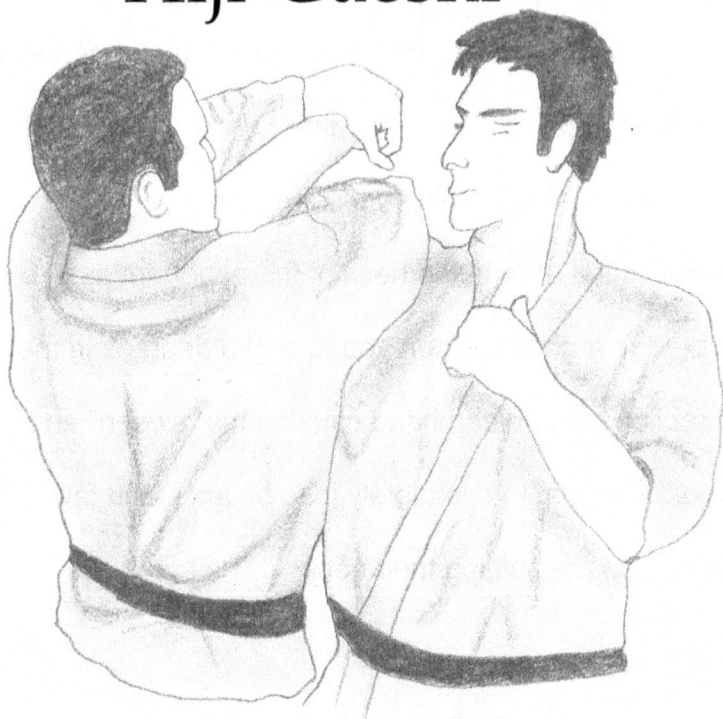

❖ **Hiji-Osae** (Elbow to Shoulder Lock) **(Green Belt)**

Hiji-Osae

❖ Juji-Uke Hiji Makikomi (X Block Restraining Lock) **Red Belt)**

1

2

❖ **Ebi-Garami** (Guillotine Choke) **(Red Belt)**

In the Ebi-Garami or Guillotine Choke, the opponent is held within the lock created by the arm constricting the neck by grabbing the opposite wrist, causing the opponent to feel discomfort. The completion of this technique is applied by arching your back causing your opponent to instantaneously submit.

The defense is to extend their arm over your back preventing you from being able to arch your back.

Although the opponent feels discomfort, until you are able to arch your back, you cannot complete the technique. The opponent can extend one arm over your back while pushing upwards with their body and pulling your arm and hand away from your opposite wrist. This would pry open your lock around their neck.

The opponent could also attempt a Kosoto-Gake while you are holding their neck. The feeling of falling would make you instinctively release their neck because you would try to break your fall. This is involuntary.

❖ **Hadaka-Jime** (Front Naked Choke) **(Red Belt)**

Hadaka-Jime

Throws & Takedowns

❖ **Tai-Otoshi** (Body Drop) **(Yellow Belt)**

Tai-Otoshi

O-Soto-Gari

This technique was adapted by Jigoro Kano for his new style Judo, from the Kito Ryu which specialized in such throwing techniques.

O-Soto-Gari

❖ **Kosoto Gake** (Outside Hook Trip)
   (Orange Belt)

If your opponent has their left leg forward and they

are in a front stance, insert your right leg and foot

behind the opponent's left leg and foot. This results

in the opponent's foot becoming trapped. Next, begin pulling the left arm of the opponent with your right hand and then push the opponent's right shoulder to your right with your left arm.

❖ **Te-Guruma** (Scoop Throw)
   (Orange Belt)

Lower your level, enter outside the opponent's lead or jab hand at an angle, grab the opponent's leg with both arms, push up and out while turning in towards the opponent. The key is using your speed and momentum to generate the power for this technique.

Te-Guruma

* **Morote-Komi-Hiza** (Double Leg Pull Sweep)
(Orange Belt)

In contrast to Te-Guruma or Scoop Throw

where you project and use your momentum to push the opponent off balance, in the Morote-Komi-Hiza or Double Leg Pull Sweep, you use pure ju or yielding by applying leverage to the opponent's knees throwing them off balance. You first lower your level by bending your knees and hips, (bending down) while grabbing behind the knees of the opponent. Second, you pull up your arms (as if lifting a wheelbarrow) while moving your momentum slightly forward and driving your chest in to the opponent, forcing them onto their back.

❖ **Uchi-Mata** (Inner Reap) **(Blue Belt)**

The Jujitsuka breaks the opponent's balance by pushing the leg between the legs of the opponent thereby dividing their fulcrum, while pushing and pulling the arms of the opponent.

- ❖ **Ko-Ouchi Gari** (Inside Hook Trip) **(Blue Belt)**

- ❖ **O-Guruma** (Outer Reap) **(Green Belt)**

- ❖ **Te-Hiza-Guruma** (Knee Wheel) **(Green Belt)**

- ❖ **Morote-Gari** (Double Leg Takedown) **(Red Belt)**

Morote-Gari

- ❖ **Ippon-Seoi-Nage** (One Arm Hip Throw) **(Red Belt)**

- ❖ **Morote-Seoi-Nage** (Lifting Hip Throw) **(Red Belt)**

The opponent is pulled over the back of the Jujitsuka and hurled towards the ground as the Jujitsuka pulls while bending over.

Ground Techniques

In Full Mount

- ❖ **Gyaku-Juji-Jime** (Reverse cross choke) **(Yellow Belt)**

After establishing the grips around the sides of the neck, the practitioner bends and drops his/her body weight and both forearms towards the ground. This tightens the choke.

Ude-Nodo-Jime (Forearm Throat Choke) **(Yellow Belt)**

By grabbing the inside of the opponent's right lapel

with your right hand, forcing the blade of your forearm across the throat of the opponent, while applying your body weight, you cause the opponent to submit.

Ude-Garami (Kimura) **(Orange Belt)**

UDE-GARAMI

Guard Types

Closed Legs Guard (Yellow Belt)

Closed Legs Guard

In the Closed Legs Guard, you are controlling your opponent's body by locking your legs around their waist. You are holding their arms from the outside to prevent them from striking you. It is important to keep your legs locked above the opponent's hips in order to maintain control.

Open Legs Guard
(Yellow Belt)

In the Opens Legs Guard your legs are open giving

you the opportunity to attempt sweeps, joint locking techniques, and escapes.

Inside Legs Guard
(Orange Belt)

In the Inside Legs Guard, your legs are bent, held together, and positioned in between the legs of the opponent which disrupts their balance by diving their fulcrum.

Maneuver Guard
(Blue Belt)

In the Maneuver Guard, you legs are working independently to stop advances from the opponent. The left leg will, for example, be bent with the foot stopping the right arm of the (your left) opponent from punching, your right leg will be straight or slightly bent and pressing on the opponent's left hip (your right) disrupting their balance.

Key Ground Escapes

Escape from Closed Legs Guard

Escape from Side Mount

Escape from Full Mount

Escape from Backmount

Opponent in Full Mount

In this position, the opponent is straddling your chest in full mount position which is a very dangerous position because the opponent can easily strike your face and apply Shime-waza or Kansetsu-waza.

Bridge & Roll Sweep (Yellow Belt)

In Bridge & Roll Sweep, if sweeping to the right, with your left hand grab the opponent's left lapel (gi collar) and with your right hand grab the opponent's left arm at the wrist or elbow. Position your right foot on the outside of the opponent's left ankle to form a base when sweeping. With your right hand pull the

opponent's left arm while pushing your left hand to

your right side while bridging your hips and rolling out.

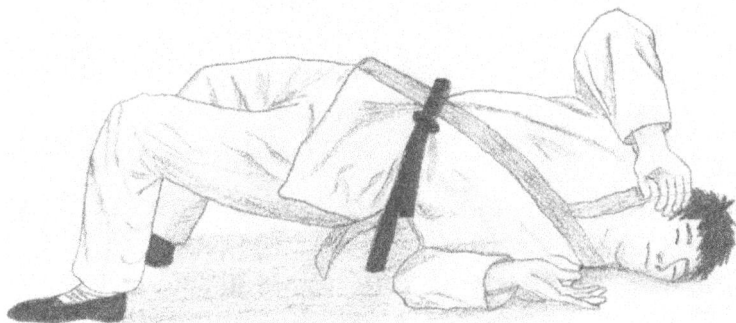

Empi-Hiza-Barai – Elbow Knee Escape
(Yellow Belt)

Using your elbows, you push away the opponent

while pulling your hips out from underneath the

opponent. This allows you time to move the opponent

in to your Open Legs Guard, Closed Legs Guard, or

Maneuver Guard.

Goshi-Barai (Hip Push Sweep) **(Blue Belt)**

Goshi-Barai

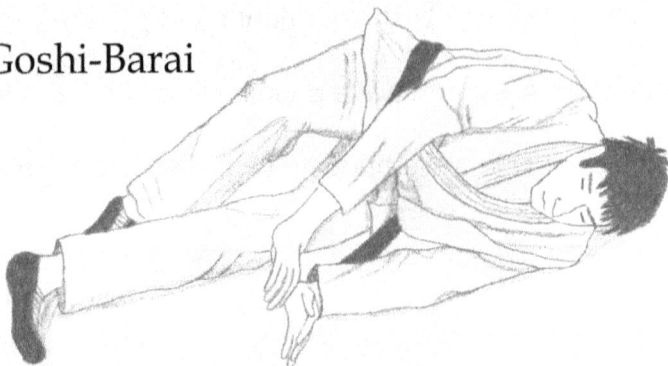

In Goshi-Barai, if sweeping your opponent to your left, use your left and right hands to push your opponent's hips back and to the left while shifting your hips to the right. This results in off balancing the opponent and providing the gap for you to pull your hips out from underneath your opponent.

Ashi-Garami-Barai (Foot Lock Sweep) (Green Belt)

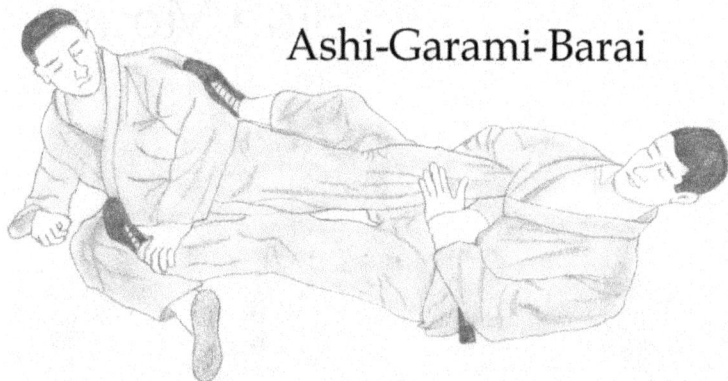

Ashi-Garami-Barai

When the opponent is in full mount position straddling your chest, shift a bit to the right and with your right foot press against your opponent's left part of the rib cage. This pushes the opponent off of you giving you time to grab his leg to apply a foot lock. By arching your back, you increase the amount of force applied to the opponent's leg and foot.

In Side Mount

Side Mount

In Side Mount position, you want to keep your knees and elbows tucked in snug against both sides of the opponent's ribs. Although this position is not painful for the opponent, this is frustrating. The opportunities to strike and attempt Kansetsu-Waza or joint locking and Shime-Waza or choking/strangulation techniques are numerous.

Uke-Gatame (Knee on stomach) **(Yellow Belt)**

Uke-Gatame

Full Mount Entry (Yellow Belt)

When you are positioned in Side Mount, you will

attempt to move to a full mount position by using your

arm that is closest to the opponent's legs and push

your forearm down above his knees to prevent his

knees from stopping or striking your face. You then

proceed to swing your leg, that is closest to the

opponent's legs, around the opponent's body,

straddling the opponent between their navel and their

solar plexus. Your knees should be firmly and tightly placed around the sides of the opponent's body, from their chest to their hips, so as to create a stable base for launching joint-locking and choking techniques.

Ude Garami (Kimura) (Orange Belt)

In Opponent's Guard in Top Mount

Full Mount Entry **(Yellow Belt)**

Tomoe-Hishigi (Stacking) **(Yellow Belt)**

Side Mount Entry **(Orange Belt)**

Kakato-Garami (Heel Lock) **(Green Belt)**

Hiza-Garami (Knee Lock) **(Red Belt)**

Hiza-Garami

Guard Bottom Position

The guard bottom position is a defensive position but

your opponent still retains the advantageous position

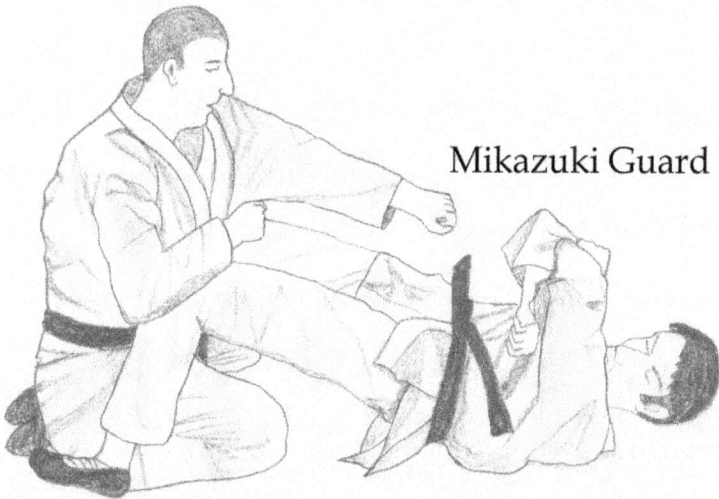

Mikazuki Guard

of being able to strike you, easier than you are able to

strike them. The key is to remain evasive and keep

moving, as staying stationary makes you vulnerable

to strikes in a real fight. The more you move, the

more opportunities are created for you to attempt joint

locking techniques, choking/strangling techniques,

sweeps, and escapes. There are two major principles

when grappling on the ground; either keep the opponent very close to you so that they are unable to punch you with any effectiveness or keep the opponent away from you at a distance that puts you out of their punching range. By bridging the hips, while in a open or closed guard (depends on the length of your legs) you are able to effectively keep the opponent from being able to strike your face. The key is to absorb or deflect. When you are holding the opponent's left and right arm so that they cannot strike you and you are holding the opponents body in your closed guard (your feet should be crossed!), the opponent is not only able to strike you but they are also in a frustrating position. The opponent is in a seemingly advantageous position but unable to strike, which frustrates the opponent, thus giving you an opportunity to attempt escapes, reversals/sweeps, or to create time and space for you to attempt a joint

locking or choking technique.

❖ **Juji-Gatame** (Cross side Arm Bar)
(Yellow Belt)

Juji-Gatame

Juji-Gatame or Cross Side Arm Bar has been

adapted from Jujitsu by styles ranging from Judo,

BJJ, Shooto, and Mixed Martial Arts. There is

little chance of escape once the opponent has

been placed in this position.

- ❖ **Uke-Gatame** (Knee on Chest) **(Yellow Belt)**

- ❖ **Ebi-Garami** (Guillotine Choke) **(Orange Belt)**

- ❖ **Ude-Guruma-Jime** (Forearm Winding Choke) **(Orange Belt)**

- ❖ **Hadaka-Jime** (Front Naked Choke)**(Blue Belt)**

- ❖ **Kakato-Garami** (Heel Hook) **(Green Belt)**

- ❖ **Sankaku- Jime** (Triangle Choke) **(Red Belt)**

Sankaku-Jime

The Sankaku-Jime or Triangle Choke is a

vital element of the Jujitsuka's arsenal of

ground grappling techniques or Ne-Waza.

Pulling down on the top of the head of the opponent after trapping the arm of the opponent results in constricting the flow of oxygen forcing the opponent to "tap-out" or pass out.

Opponent in Your Guard Sweeps

❖ **Os-Barai** Push Knee Sweep **(Orange Belt)**

In Os-Barai, if sweeping to your left, position the bottom of your left foot snug against the opponent's right knee (your left). With your right hand, grab the right lapel of the opponent, with your left hand grab the opponent's right arm at the elbow or wrist holding their arm, in against the side of your body. Simultaneously push the opponent to your left with your right hand that is holding the opponent's right lapel, pulling the opponent's right arm with your left hand, while extending your left foot resting against the opponent's right knee causing the opponent to lose balance and turn. Your right leg should swing around the side of the opponent, with the end result being you are either in or nearly in, the opponent's full mount with you straddling their chest.

❖ **Guruma-Barai** (Wheel Sweep) **(Orange Belt)**

In the Guruma-Barai, to sweep your opponent to your left, insert your right foot under the left side of the left thigh (your right) of the opponent, grab the left lapel of the opponent's gi with your right hand and grab the opponent's right arm at the elbow or wrist with your left hand, turn on to your left side (shifting your body weight) while raising the opponent's knee (in which you placed your foot) in a wheel fashion back towards your left shoulder. You should be pulling the opponent's right arm with your left hand and pushing the opponent to the left side with your right hand that

is holding their lapel.

* **Sutemi-Barai** (Overhead Sweep) **(Blue Belt)**

Sutemi-Barai

* **Te-Ashi-Barai (Hand to Ankle Sweep)
(Blue Belt)**

As the opponent moves higher into your guard, their ankles become vulnerable to grabs. The key is to grab both ankles, and bridge your body (shifting your body weight to the left side) causing the opponent to fall.

- ❖ **Mikazuki-Barai** (Crescent Sweep) **(Green Belt)**

In the Mikazuki Sweep, if you are sweeping your opponent to your right (their left), grab the opponent's left lapel (your right) with your left hand and grab the opponent's left arm at the elbow with your right hand. Slightly turn your body to the right and position your right leg and foot firmly against the left leg of the opponent. Your left leg and foot should be stationed under the armpit of the opponent. You should simultaneously turn your body completely to the right (so that your right ear is parallel with the floor) while pushing your right leg against the side of the opponent's left leg and pulling the opponent to your right (his left) with your leg and foot which is positioned under his right armpit.

❖ **Kama-Barai (Green Belt)**

Kama-Barai

❖ **Hiza-Barai (Knee Sweep) (Red Belt)**

Opponent in Side Mount

When the opponent is in your side mount position, turn your entire body **towards** your opponent while pushing him/her away using your arms and elbows. The purpose of this is to create enough to space to move the opponent in to your closed legs guard. This is defensive and aims to "shutdown" and frustrate the attacks of the opponent.

- ❖ Roll In **(Yellow Belt)**
- ❖ Roll out **(Blue Belt)**

Self Defense/Escape Techniques

- ❖ Front Bear Hug with free arms Escape **(Yellow Belt)**

- ❖ Full Nelson Escape **(Yellow Belt)**

- ❖ Back Clinch Escape **(Yellow Belt)**

- ❖ Collar Grab Escape **(Orange Belt)**

- ❖ Shoulder Grab Escape **(Orange Belt)**

- ❖ Wrist Grab Escape **(Orange Belt)**

- ❖ Side Headlock Escape **(Blue Belt)**

- ❖ Guillotine Escape **(Green Belt)**

- ❖ Rear Naked Choke Escape **(Green Belt)**

Standing Rear Naked Choke Defense

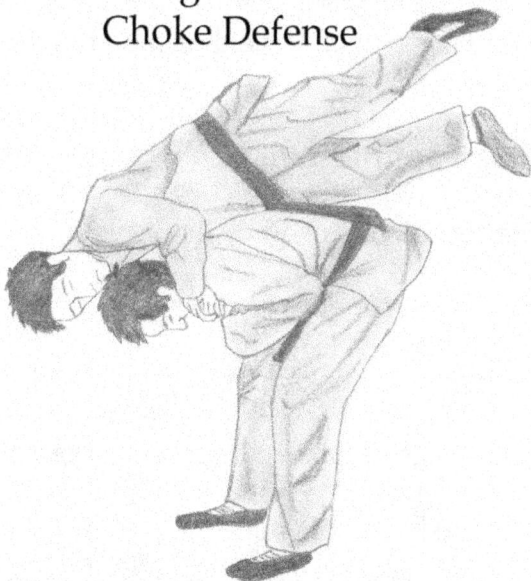

The key is to act quickly. If the opponent

holding the naked choke tightens their lock, the
possibility that you will become unconscious in
under seven seconds is likely and probable. Pull
down with both hands on the opponent's forearm
and bend over as if attempting to touch your
hands to the floor. If done quickly, the opponent
will catapult over your back.

❖ Sprawl Escape **(Green Belt)**

❖ Bear Hug with arms held escape **(Red Belt)**

Punching Techniques

The techniques used by the Jujitsu
practicioner in free fighting mode and clinch are the
jab, reverse punch, hook, uppercut, and the lunging
jab. The jab is used to keep opponents from entering
closer than the length of your extended jab, thus
creating time and space for you to maneuver.

The reverse punch is the most important punch and is to be used following the jab. Punches as a general rule, should always be in combinations and are usually followed by a kicking technique.

The lunging punch is a striking technique that is used when you are outside the kicking and punching range of the opponent. The lunging punch allows you to close the space between you and the opponent and is usually followed by a clinch or off balancing.

Always remember to relax your muscles as you are punching. Do not clinch up your shoulders or tense your neck muscles. It is important to use fast retraction or pulling back of your arm after delivering a punch. Make sure to transfer the power of your body in to the punch, by rotating your hips with your knees bent slightly.

Blocking Techniques

❖ Mikazuki Guard

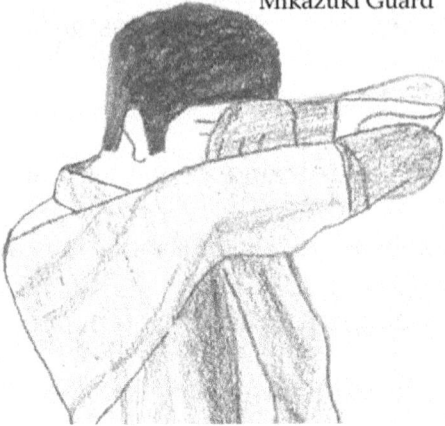

Mikazuki Guard

Used to block high-level jabs, high-level reverse punches, and high-level kicks. It is vulnerable to the uppercut punch from near.

❖ **Boxing Guard** – Elbows raised and tucked in 2-3 inches apart, fists are held close together, and kept beneath eye level.

❖ **Jodan-Uke** (High Forearm Block)

Used to block strikes to the head including

reverse punches, axe kicks, crescent kicks,

and weapon attacks to the head.

Jodan-Uke

❖ **Chodan-Uke** (Outside Forearm Block)

Used to block jabs, reverse punches, mid-level

roundhouse kicks, mid-level front kicks, mid-

level sidekicks.

❖ **Gedan-Uke** (Downward Block)

Used to block low roundhouse kicks and low

front kicks.

Kicking Techniques

Proper and effective kicking starts with

constant practicing. The power of each kick not only

comes from the legs, but more importantly the hips. It

is the strength and rotation of the hips that generate

the power.

❖ **Mae-Geri** (Front Kick)

The key to generating strength is to

raise your knee as high as possible before

delivering your front kick. At the same time

you deliver your front kick, arch your back to

generate greater power. The front kick is

useful when an attacker is rushing towards

you. Wait until the attacker is within range of your front kick, raise your knee high, snap the kick in to the vital parts of the attacker, (groin, stomach, knees) striking with the ball of the foot, and then recoil or pull back your leg. There are two variations of the front kick, the push kick, and the snap kick. In the application of the snap kick, your leg and knee raise up to your solar plexus, the leg straightens, (slowly tensing the muscle) snapping the kick out and striking the opponent's stomach with the ball of your foot. The leg is slightly tensed and is for the most part loose, until the point of contact in which the quadriceps muscles are tightened, thereby generating power. After the delivery of the snap front kick, the Jujitsuka rapidly recoils and retracts the striking leg.

- ❖ **Hiza Geri** (Knee strike)

The Hiza-Geri is very effective when in

clinch mode and within punching range.

Knees can be delivered to the stomach,

groin, thighs, ribs, and face of the opponent.

It is recommended to keep your boxing guard up or

Mikazuki Guard, to prevent your opponent from

striking you, when you enter their punching range.

- ❖ **Mawashi Geri** (Roundhouse Kick)

GEDAN MAWASHI GERI

The Low Roundhouse kick or Gedan Mawashi

Geri is an effective tool for delivering kicks at a

range which keeps you away from your

opponent's punching range. The key to delivering

effective low roundhouse kicks is to first, pull up

the ball of the front foot and pivot your front foot

towards the outside of your stance, while twisting

the hips and striking the opponent's thigh with

the instep of your foot.

The power of the low roundhouse kick is generated from the hips not the tightening, contracting, or tensioning of your leg muscles. The key is to keep the leg that is striking, loose and not tensed. The speed of your leg plus the rotation of your hips will generate the strength. Remember to first pivot your front foot out!

❖ **Yoko Geri** (Side Kick)

❖ **Mikazuki Geri** (Crescent Kick)

Gripping/Seizing (Kumikata)

Double Under hooks Clinch **(Yellow)**

Side Clinch **(Yellow)**

Rear Clinch **(Yellow)**

Neck and Wrist Clinch **(Orange)**

Neck Clinch **(Orange)**

Neck and Inside Elbow Clinch **(Orange)**

Right Lapel/Right Outside Wrist Grip **(Blue Belt)**

Left Lapel/Left Outside Wrist Grip **(Blue Belt)**

Right Bicep/ Right Outside Wrist Grip **(Green Belt)**

Left Bicep/Left Outside Wrist Grip **(Green Belt)**

Over under Clinch **(Green Belt)**

Understanding Grips

Because the principle of Ju or Yielding depends on pulling and pushing in synchronicity, the correct grips must be first established in order to be able to practice Kuzushi-no-Happo or 8 directional off balancing techniques. The incorrect placement of your hands on your opponent or your grips, will negatively affect throwing techniques you attempt. Knowing and being able to demonstrate the correct grips, is a fundamental skill in jujitsu.

Grappling Exercises

❖ 8 Directional Off balancing (Happo No Kuzushi)

❖ Defending the Takedown

❖ Entering for the Clinch

Attack Strategies

❖ **DEHANA WAZA** – Punching or kicking the opponent as they move.

❖ **SUTEMI** – This is a sacrifice technique which means you will probably get hit, but be able to deliver a technique immediately after.

❖ **GO NO SEN** – Attacking after being attacked

❖ **OI WAZA** – Follow up strikes during opponent's retreat

- ❖ **DEBANA** – Window of opportunity to attempt a technique, during opponent's attack.

Mental Strategies

- ❖ **FUDOSHIN**- Immovable mind, calm spirit

- ❖ **MUSHIN**- No mind; To not be effected by your surroundings, clearing your mind of thoughts

- ❖ **FUSHIN**- Frozen or stopped mind.

8 Directions of Off Balancing or Kuzushi No Happo

Off balancing is vital to starting the process of throwing your opponent. Failure to use off balancing may result in the failure of the execution of the throw. The key is to beginning off balancing before you start your throw. By using your own body weight and momentum, you are able to definitively affect the balance of the opponent.

KUZUSH-NO-HAPPO

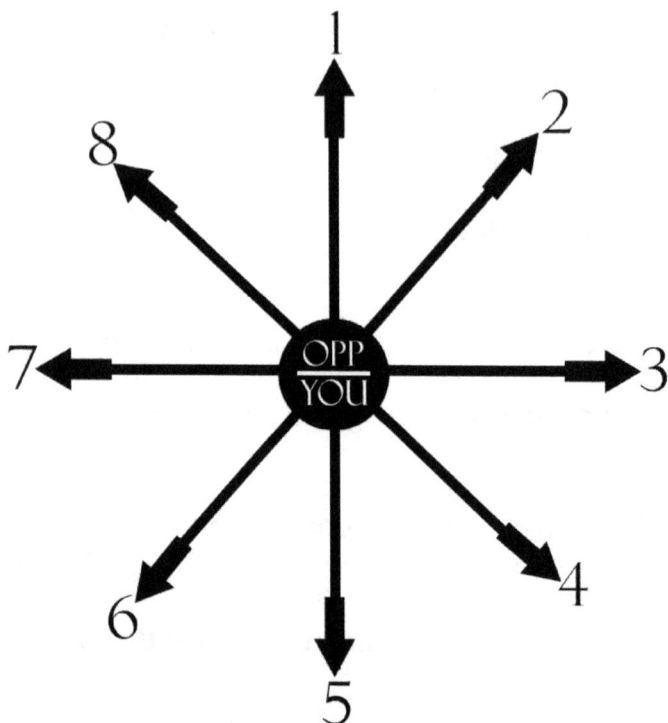

By training constantly in the applications of Kuzushi-no-happo, you are training the "muscle memory" of your arms and hands as they grip the opponent. You are training your legs to position themselves properly, and you're training your body to move in the eight directions that will off balance your opponent. These are the main aspects to learn to use

Kuzushi effectively. Moving in the direction of or away from the opponent while pushing and pulling is one of the simplest ways of applying Kuzushi.

The most effective way to apply the principle of yielding is by entering and moving into your opponent when you are being pulled and turning away from your opponent when you are being pushed. Kuzushi means to break the opponents balance. The use of off balancing prevents you from having to rely on strength rather than technique, especially because there is a good chance your opponent may be stronger than you. Striking is also an off balancing method because the strike, whether punch or kick, creates disruption for a short amount of time, giving the jujitsu practitioner time to initiate an attack. Only after the striking techniques have been effective in

Kuzushi no happo

disrupting the concentration of the opponent will a

throwing technique be applied. Individuals are

either lifted or pulled. In essence, there are only two

ways to off balance an individual when grappling.

You can either force the opponent to fall over the ball of their feet by leaning forward or fall back over their heels by leaning backward.

Whether the opponent's thrown over the ball of their feet or being thrown back over their heels, they are being off balanced and setup for the jujitsu practitioner to enter for positioning their body properly to effectively execute the throw. The Tsukure is the movement of positioning your body so that you will be able to execute a throwing technique with effectiveness. The completion of the technique is Kake and is related to the first principle that says maximum gain with minimum effort. By the simple use of leverage, a tall heavy man can be lifted and pushed if the application of technique is correct. In order to properly apply the technique, the use of Kuzushi will allow you to move much heavier and stronger opponents without having to rely on strength.

Taking the Initiative

I.   Sen Sen No Sen (Superior Initiative)

This is similar to chess in that your aim and

ultimate goal is to be able to be able to intelligently

predict the next strike or technique that the

opponent will attempt against you. The prevention

of conflict, relies on preventing the creation of

conflict or stopping conflict before it escalates.

Based on the stance and positioning of the

opponent, you should be able to read their

defensive gaps and predict their next offensive

move.

II. Sen (Initiative)

This is to foil the offensive move or attack of the

opponent by attacking the instant before the attack is started. This is not a pre-emptive strike but rather simultaneous defense.

III. Ato No Sen (Initiative in Defense)

In this state, the defense is started after the offensive technique has started, but before the offensive technique has been executed.

The attitude should be to take the initiative in defending oneself without falling victim to the opponent's attacks. In Ato No Sen, the jujitsuka should never allow the opponent to control and take the initiative thereby setting the pace. The jujitsu practicioner should use all techniques available to control the opponent while thinking constantly and gauging the level of force that is being used.

Scoring System

Strikes - 1 Point is awarded for strikes that land to body, legs, torso. Strikes to the face are not allowed.

Throws - 2 Points are awarded for successful Throws and 1/2 Point for each Throw Attempt

Side Mount Position - 1 Point is awarded for successful Side Mount Position. No points are awarded for attempts.

Top Mounted Position - 2 Points are awarded for successful Top Mount Position. No points are awarded for attempts.

Escapes/Reversals - 2 Points are awarded for each successful escape/reversal. No points are awarded for attempts.

Submissions - Successful submission ends match

but Jujitsuka receives ½ point for each attempt.

Rules

Matches are 3 Rounds, 5 minutes per Round. No biting, eye gouging, fish hooking, spinal submissions, neck cranks, and/or disrespectful behavior are allowed. The most points accumulated after 3 Rounds or the first to force the opponent in to submission is the winner.

Kata and Randori

Jujitsu practitioners use kata and randori for learning. Kata is a set of pre-defined movements that enable students to learn techniques and train their muscle memory.

Randori or free sparring, is a controlled form of sparring that creates an environment which enables the practitioners to learn safely, without the risk of serious injuries, while allowing the practitioners to apply the techniques they have learned. In the near past, many martial artists had the notion that "real" martial arts techniques were too dangerous to be practiced and that its practice could result in paralysis or death. It was soon proved that this belief and philosophy was not only incorrect, but highly invalid. When these same martial artists faced opponents that had trained in free sparring or randori, they were easily defeated. How are techniques that are "too dangerous" practiced? They are not practiced because they are dangerous, hence the reason for the creation of sport jujitsu and the removal of techniques that could not be practiced at ½ speed.

Kata's benefits include increase in internal energy or Ki, increase in blood flow /circulation creating higher levels of bodily oxygen which theoretically increases the human longevity.

Fighting Methods

❖ **Constant Circling** - Maneuvering by circling around the weak side of the individual's front arm.

❖ **Attack in Combinations** - Students are taught to strike or attempt submissions in 3 move combinations. Black Belts are required to use 5-6 move combinations for example; jab, reverse punch, low round house kick, off balancing, throwing, joint locking and/or choking/strangulation techniques are performed in synchronicity.

❖ **Counter-striking** - Using and taking advantage of openings and gaps created by the opponent.

Sparring Tips

Miyamoto Musashi, master swordsman said "The true science of martial arts means practicing them in such a way that they will be useful at any time". **(5)**

- Practice reading the defenses of your opponent and be able to recognize gaps in their defense.

- Use strikes, off balancing, and throws in combinations when in free fighting and clinch.

- Take any gap your opponent gives you; if your opponent is within range for your kick, then deliver it. Do not wait until you are in his punching range.

- Breath and pace yourself until the opponent reveals a gap for you to exploit.

- Do not allow your opponent to outmaneuver you. Control the pace.

- Do not drop your defense or unnecessarily reveals gaps in your defense.   Use the Mikazuki Guard protects the face from elbows, hooks, crosses, jabs, reverse punches, and kicks.

UNDERSTANDING RANGE

Understanding range is essential for the Jujitsu practitioner because every successful execution of a technique, whether punch, kick, throw, joint locking technique, choking technique, or sweep, depends on range. So what is range? Range is the area that your attacks have effect on your opponent. Your range, is the area in which your techniques can be executed on your opponent. Then there is your "opponents range", which is the area that your opponent's techniques can be executed on you.

FOR EXAMPLE

If your right leg including your right foot is a total of four feet long from the hip and if your opponent enters to four feet of you, your opponent is now within your kicking range and can be roundhouse kicked with your right leg. If your opponent steps closer than four feet, your roundhouse kick to the opponent's outer thigh will be less successful because, a closer opponent means less axis and less force for your kick. A closer opponent you are striking with a roundhouse kick, also means you are not striking using the instep of the foot, which can also cause injuries to your leg, besides not being able to deliver as much force as a roundhouse kick delivered to an opponent at exactly 4 foot range. Although many "mixed martial artists" disavow range, the use of range is vital for defending and attacking. An opponent 1-2 feet from you is susceptible to front kicks, jabs, reverse punches, and entries for throws and submissions.

DIFFERENT RANGES

- ❖ PUNCHING RANGE
- ❖ KICKING RANGE
- ❖ OFF BALANCING & THROWING RANGE

UNDERSTANDING TIMING

Timing is the opportunity given to you by your opponent to deliver strikes. Every technique in the arsenal of a Jujitsu practitioner can only be delivered at the "time" that it can be delivered. For example, you cannot strike, attempt a throw or submission where there is no opening or gap provided to you by the opponent.

5 GRAPPLING TIPS

1. **Be Agile** – Don't move sluggishly

2. **Train safely** – Always use grappling gloves and interlocking thick mats.

3. **Practicing training at different speeds** – Train entering, gripping, and clinching at ½ speed and full speed.

4. **Avoid injuries & Tap Three Times** – Tap three times to signal you have submitted. Your ego might tell you that you can keep going, but risking bodily harm to yourself is worse. Many individuals in fighting and combat systems that lack the traditional martial arts code of respect

and honor, will refuse to tap. Not tapping will cause serious injuries and is considered negligent and dangerous behavior. Many have had to have back surgery and other operations to attempt to reverse the damage done by training under a martial arts style and instructor that was more driven by competition rather than the safety needs of the practitioners.

5. **Always respect your training partner** - Train at speeds and intensity levels that are comfortable for your training partner. Also, if your training partner is not responding to verbal requests for slowing down and using less strength, the Sempai or Senior Student should be notified immediately to prevent injuries from occurring.

How to Defeat a Boxer

Boxers are highly skilled fighters and they are accustomed to taking blows to deliver blows. Boxers are also trained to fighting in Clinch mode, so the best strategy would be to keep your distance from their punching range. Although you may be far more skilled in ground grappling than a boxer, it would be a mistake to take the fight to the ground. First, the ground is most likely not soft and cushiony like the tatami in a Dojo and will probably be concrete. Second, the boxer may not be alone, leaving you vulnerable to attacks from his compatriots while you are on the ground.

1. **Evasive** - Stay away from a boxer's main weapons, their hands.

2. **Be Cautious** - Never ever drop your Mikazuki Guard or any guard you are defending with. Boxers become very frustrated when they have no gaps to exploit. This causes the boxer to make mistakes giving you opportunities(gaps) to exploit.

3. **Work the Legs** - Strike with low roundhouse kicks to the opponents thighs and front kicks to the opponent's knees and groin as soon as the boxer enters your kicking range.

4. **Front Kicks** - If the boxer gets so close that you are in the boxer's punching range, immediately deliver front kicks to the boxer's knees and groin.

How to Defeat a Wrestler

1. **Be Agile** - Be fast on your feet because wrestlers drop their hips low and shoot in.

2. **Use throwing techniques** - Although wrestlers are skilled in throwing, their style is far different than throws using "ju" or yielding. Use of Kuzushi-no-happo to disrupt their balance. Use trips, sweeps, inner reaps, outer reaps, and takedowns to frustrate your opponent.

3. **Use Joint Locking Techniques** - Be generous in the amount of Kansetsu-Waza or joint locking techniques you apply. Remember to use these techniques in combination, fluidly moving from one

submission attempt to the next.

How to Defeat a Mixed Martial Artist

Mixed martial artists are individuals that have trained in multiple martial arts including boxing, wrestling, jujitsu, etc.

1. **Find their Weakness** – Mixed martial artists have trained in boxing, kicking, grappling, submissions, etc. but are nonetheless more trained in one background. Many mixed martial artist come from a wrestling, bjj, karate, or boxing background. They may be strong in free fighting, but weaker in grappling, they may be proficient at ground fighting, but lack skills in throwing. They could be strong in grappling but weak in submissions. No martial artist is equally skilled

in free fighting, clinch fighting, and ground fighting. If there is such martial artist, they are most likely average in all fields. The key is to read and find their weakness and exploit them.

2. **Focus on Your Strengths** - Know your strengths. Are you a better free fighter, using kicks and punches? Are you a better grappler utilizing throws? Are you a better ground fighter utilizing submissions? It is vital for you to know the answer to these questions.

How to Defeat a Karateka

Karate practicioners are traditional martial artists and are very capable with their legs. They use an assortment of kicks that you will have to block or evade including front, roundhouse, side kicks, etc.

1. **Avoid their legs!** – Enter as fast as possible

within the kicking range and move to a clinch.
Use off balancing, throws, and trips to take
them to the ground.

2. **Use Shime & Kansetsu Waza** – Use your
knowledge of choking & joint locking
techniques to end the match without the need
for endless striking.

How to Fight Multiple Attackers

The key to fighting and surviving an attack from
multiple individuals is the following:

1. **Line them up** – Move towards each attacker,
in essence, lining them up so that your back or
your sides are not exposed.

2. **Timing is essential** – Buy time for yourself by
using front kicks, off balancing, and throws to

create time and space between the opponent you are facing and the next opponent, 3-4 seconds away from attacking you.

3. **Do Not Fall!** – Do not use high kicks or any kick, that will make you lose your balance. Front kicks are *more* stable than other kicks used in training. If you fall, you become vulnerable to street objects being broken over your head, so immediately roll out and stand up.

4. **No Fancy Moves** – Stick to the fundamentals; punching combinations, front kicks, off balancing, and throwing.

5. **Work Fast!** – Most fights end in under a few minutes, so work fast! In fact, the faster and more energetically you fight, the more

intimidated your attackers will be to continue.

IMPORTANT JUJITSU SCHOOLS (KORYU OR TRADITIONAL)

❖ **Kito Ryu** – Specialized in Kuzushi-no-happo and Nage-Waza

FAMOUS PRACTICIONER:
Jigoro Kano

❖ **Takenouchi-Ryu** – Specialized in Osae-Waza or Control Techniques

FAMOUS PRACTICIONER:
Takenouchi Hisamori

❖ **Yoshin Ryu** – Specialized in Atemi-Waza

FAMOUS PRACTICIONER:
Akiyama Shirobei Yoshitoki

❖ **Fusen Ryu** – Specialized in Ne-Waza

FAMOUS PRACTICIONER:
Yukio Tani

- ❖ **Daito Ryu Aiki-Jujitsu** – Specialized in Atemi Waza, Kansetsu-Waza, & Nage Waza

FAMOUS PRACTICIONER
Takeda Sokaku

Is Jujitsu Japanese in Origin?

There has been much discussion recently regarding the origins of jujitsu or jiu-jitsu as some refer to it. Some martial arts scholars have stated that jujitsu originated in ancient Iran, India, China, Russia, and other parts of the world. According to David Mitchell, sumo and jujitsu shared common origins stemming back to the 8th century, but the split became apparent by the 15th century when Japan was embroiled with civil strife **(3)**. Patrick McCarthy in his translated version of the Bubishi, the ancient Chinese martial arts manual, stated that Chen Yuanbin known as Chin Gempei in Japanese, taught his art of jujitsu to Fukuno Shichiroemon, Miura

Yokiemon, and Isogai Jirozaemon who ended up creating three new jujitsu schools**(4)**. Charles Yerkow in his 1942 work "Modern Judo" stated that jujitsu originated in Tibet , was passed onto China, and eventually found its way to Japan**(6)**. The fact that all cultures have a martial legacy is undisputable and the number of ways that a body can be manipulated is limited. The "shared conditions" theory extolled in Brazilian Jujitsu champion Renzo Gracie's "Mastering Jujitsu" is a valid theory **(7)**. The "shared conditions" theory states that the necessity for the invention and creation of fighting arts was essential due to the harsh conditions in which humans lived. Irving Hancock in his seminal work on jujitsu, "Jiu-jitsu Combat Tricks" stated that strangleholds, chokeholds, and techniques related, were part of ancient Japanese culture and had evolved in to jujitsu**(8)**. It's also widely believed that Chin Gempin brought Jujitsu in the form of Kenpo to Japan from China in the mid 1600's. This is questionable because grappling events had been held publicly in Japan since 23 B.C. David Mitchell stated in the Overlook Martial Arts Handbook that jujitsu stems from 15th century Japan**(9)**. According to Darrel Max Craig's book Japan's Ultimate Martial Art, Shinra Suburo Yoshimitsu created Daito Ryu Aiki-Jujitsu which lead to the creation of further offshoot styles**(10)**.

Fusen Ryu Jujitsu was founded by master Motsuge Zenji and was the 9th descendant of Daimyo Takeda Shingen **(11)**. Its star student, Mataemon Tanabe, challenged and defeated Kodokan Judoka multiple times. Jigoro Kano was a devoted jujitsu student and he placed emphasis on throwing techniques because the school of jujitsu which he attended specialized in throwing techniques. Jigoro's Judo borrowed the name Judo from Kito-Ryu Judo, which was the first jujitsu school to ever use the term. Jigoro Kano, an educator and jujitsu student of master Hachinosuke Fukuda of the Tensjo-Shinyo school, went on to create Judo. There were much jujitsu schools that specialized in completely different curriculums. One school was famous for Ne-Waza and another for compliance and arrest techniques.

It can be argued that jujitsu is Japanese because the root words which the word is based on, attest to its Nihon origins. The word "ju" in Japanese means yielding. The word "jitsu" in Japanese means art. The samurai of Japan during the civil war like Sengoku Jedai period depended on the use of jujitsu to defeat an armed opponent when they were

The Samurai carried two
    weapons in to battle

unarmed.   This is specifically the reason that

jujitsu was not a "Do" or a way, but rather an amalgamation of techniques designed for the sole purpose of effectiveness. The samurai was a term used for men of noble lineage that were assigned to guard members of the Japanese Imperial Court. **(12)** The samurai grew in power and became a class of land owning nobles that became Daimyo or feudal landowners overseeing large tracts of lands. With no more wars to fight, the subjugation of the samurai class to the government, and the modernization programs of the Meiji government, the retired samurai were "encouraged" to work in occupations such as farming and commerce. Inazo Nitobe in his work "Bushido" stated that after the samurai fief lands were seized, the samurai moved towards commerce, but only one from every one hundred had success in these commercial endeavors**(13)**. Carrying swords was now a crime against the state. Former Samurai who broke the rules were publicly humiliated and chastised for their "backwardness" or lack of progressive attitudes. Jujitsu practitioners, who were former samurai, developed a negative reputation. The gradual and real change in the cultural norms relating to jujitsu took shape. Many chose to open a dojo or a place of the way. These schools were meant to instill martial and spiritual qualities within the practitioner. These schools also had official permission or were safe from persecution by the government. Former samurai such as Sokaku Takeda of Daito Ryu Aiki-Jujitsu became teachers. The growth and popularity of jujitsu was undoubtedly influenced by media but the evolution and growth of modern Jujitsu took place in gyms, garages, and backyards internationally. The Japanese evolutionary development of the various schools of jujitsu has left a legacy of styles ranging from Judo, Jujitsu, Submission Grappling, Aikido, and others. Jujitsu retains the traditional cultural mannerisms, the effectiveness and combat value for which jujitsu was created, while practicing the "art" in the form of a sport. Sport Jujitsu has reached a mass audience and is now an official World Games sport. The creation of Aikido was by Moriheba Ueshiba, a student of Sokaku Takeda. Sokaku Takeda was famous for his vigilant style in dealing with criminals and was popular for training officials in jujitsu. According to John Stevens, author of Abundant Peace, the biography of Morihei Ueshiba, Sokaku Takeda was a short tempered ruffian that would "raid" Ueshiba's dojos attempting to take students from his pupil and would extort money from Ueshiba.**(2)** It is notable that Ueshiba was the opposite of his one-time teacher, samurai, and jujitsu master, although is it

generally accepted by many expert martial arts

scholars including John Stevens, that Ueshiba was

essentially self taught.

Samurai

Ueshiba stated that "the way of a warrior is based on

humanity, love and sincerity" thus signaling a historic shift of martial arts from life & death skills to physical and spiritual practices for the betterment of the human character **(14)**.

THE FOLLOWING IS NOT BE CONSTRUED AS LEGAL ADVICE & IT IS ADVISED FOR YOU TO ASK A LAWYER

Jujitsu & the Law

Although we are guaranteed the right to self defense and the right to protect our bodies, our families' bodies, and our employees' bodies, the amount of force used must be relevant and related to the severity of the threat the potential victim is faced with. Although you are defending yourself or your loved ones, excessive force can result in you being arrested (or being sued!). If a woman is in danger of being sexually assaulted, seriously injured, it would

not be uncommon for her to have to use more than

the necessary amount of force to stop the attack.

It can be argued that an individual who has been

trained in martial arts, has applicable knowledge of

techniques that can be deemed dangerous. The

jujitsu practicioner has the advantage in that its style

has a range of techniques that are used for controlling

the individual.

If you are attacked in your home or at your

place of business, you have no duty whatsoever to

retreat. But if you are in the street, and there is an

opportunity for you to retreat to safety, but you choose

to attack, this is deemed illegal. You can only attack

the alleged criminal perpetrator at the moment they

are going to attack you, not before or after. To attack

before, would make you the initiator and attack after

would seem like revenge. The law also protects the alleged criminal perpetrator by making illegal the use of deadly force by you, if the perpetrator was using non-deadly force.   The key is to retreat if you can and only use as much force as needed to prevent you from being the perpetrator's next victim.

Verbal Jujitsu

Verbal jujitsu is the intentional use of language to yield in a verbal confrontation with a potential attacker, while using the language of the opponent to blend with the opponent, thereby neutralizing their words, and causing them to yield or share your thoughts/ideas. Another form is using language to control or make your opponent comply without using anger or emotion.

In Confrontation with a Potential Attacker:

Diffuse - Attempt to diffuse the confrontation by not taking the bait. Not taking the bait means not responding to a verbal attack in a confrontation and re-directing the attack to confront the matter being discussed rather than the periphery or semi-peripheral issues that may be unrelated.

Compromise but Set Limits - It is honorable to compromise and back down at certain times and to give credence to the viewpoints of your opponent however, you must set verbal limits with the opponent that should not be crossed.

Keep Your Distance – Do not allow the potential attacker to get closer than 2 feet of you. This is a recipe for disaster because you can be "sucker" punched or striked without you having ample time to react. This can and will result in you being striked and becoming temporarily "stunned" for 3-5 seconds.

Stop the Issue, Stop the Confrontation – The best decision might be for you to be the "bigger" person and for you to retreat to safety(your car, a store,etc) and not engage the verbal attacks of the potential attacker.

Make Sure that There are Witnesses – If your potential attacker pulls a gun on you in the street, or in a university, or at school, there are bound to be witnesses. If the potential attacker tells you to get in the car with them or they will shoot you, it is highly unlikely that they will shoot you with witnesses(or even without witnesses) and if you enter their car, the likely that you will be sexually assaulted and murdered is high. The best thing to do is run or fight

(only if you stand a fighting chance) like your life

depended on it.

GLOSSARY

- **Ashi** – Foot

- **Ate** – Striking techniques

- **Atemi** – Striking to vital parts of the body

- **Bushido** – Way of the Warrior. Samurai code of honor.

- **Dan** – Black Belt Grade

- **Datchi** - Stance

- **Do** – Way

- **Domo Arigato** – Thank You. (Formal)

- **Garami** – Locking

- **Gatame** – Holding, Entanglement

- **Geri** – Kick

- **Gi** – Uniform

- **Goshi** - Hips

- **Goshin** – Self Defense

- **Guruma** – Wheel like motion

- **Gyaku** – Reverse

- **Hajime** - Start

- **Hiji** - Elbow

- **Jitsu/Jutsu** – Art

- **Ju** – Yielding. Soft. Gentle

- **Jujitsu Ni Sente Nashi** – There is no first attack in Jujitsu. Adopted from Funakoshi's famous saying "Karate Ni Sente Nashi".

- **Kakato** – Heel

- **Kansetsu** – Joint locking. (Arm, Leg, Shoulder)

- **Kata** - Shoulder

- **Kata** – Set of pre-defined movements that train

the practitioners muscle memory.

- **Kake** - Execution

- **Kappo** - Resuscitation

- **Kendo** – Way of the Sword

- **Kenjitsu** – Sword Techniques

- **Ki** – Inner Strength. Life Force. Internal Energy.

- **Kote** – Wrist

- **Kuzushi** – Off Balancing

- **Mataemon Tanabe** – Master of Fusen Ryu

- **Matte** – Stop

- **Mokuso** - Meditation

- **Morehei Ueshiba** – Student of Sokaku Takeda. Founded Aikido or Way of Peace

- **Miyamoto Musashi** – Self-taught master swordsman that dueled 60 times victoriously.

- **Nage** – Throwing

- **Nihon** – Japanese or Japanese origin.

- **Osae** - Control

- **Otoshi** - Drop

- **Ryu** – School

- **Seiza** – Kneeling position

- **Sempai** – Assistant Instructor. Senior Student.

- **Sensei** - Instructor

- **Shihan** – Honorific title. Not Belt Based.

- **Shime** – Choke or strangle.

- **Tatami** - Mat

- **Te** – Hand

- **Tekubi** - Wrist

- **Tori** – Attacker

- **Tsuri** - Lift

- **Tsukure** – Entry

- **Uchi** – Inside

- **Ude** - Arm

- **Uke** – Block

- **Ukemi** – Breakfalling techniques

- **Waza** – Techniques

- **Zenkutsu Datchi** – Front Stance

COUNTING

1. Ichi – pronounced eech

2. Ni – pronounced nee

3. San – pronounced sahn

4. Shi – pronounced she

5. Go – pronounced go

6. Roku – pronounced rook

7. Shichi – pronounced sheech

8. Hachi (hach)

9. Kyu (kyu)

10. Ju (joo)

Note: Count in the language which is most comfortable for you.

ANNUAL JUJITSU TOURNAMENTS

❖ USA National Ju-Jitsu & Judo Championships

Annual Date: Mid April

Contact: Dr. Ernest G. McPeek, J.D. - National
Championships Director: 1-800-676-8087

❖ Paris Open

Annual Date: Early June

Contact: COMITÉ DE LA RÉGION
ÎLE DE FRANCE DE JUDO
21-25 avenue de la Porte de Châtillon
75014 – Paris
Tel.:(+33) 01 45 41 05 70
Fax:(+33) 01 45 41 07 80
E-mail: info@idfjudo.com
Stephane Bourmeau (+33) 06 86 83 82 74
E-mail: Stephane.bourumeau@wanadoo.fr

❖ Spain Open Ju-Jitsu Championships

Annual Date: December

FEDERACION MADRILEÑA DE JUDO
Centro de Tecnificación de Judo de la Comunidad de Madrid
P.D.M. Villaviciosa de Odón
C/ León 59
28670 – Villaviciosa de Odón
MADRID
Phone: +34 902 14 20 10
Fax: +34 91 616 60 27
E-mail: promocion@fmjudo.net

REFERENCES

(1)Tsunetomo, Yamamoto. Wilson, William Scott. 1979. Hagakure; The Book of the Samurai. Pp.94 Kodansha International

(2) Ueshiba, Morihei. Stevens, John. 1987. Abundant Peace. Pp.42 Shambhala Books.

(3) Mitchell, David. 1989. Complete Book of Martial Arts. Pp.69. Gallery Books

(4) McCarthy, Patrick. 2008. Bubishi. Pp.147 Tuttle Publishing.

(5) Musashi, Miyamoto. Cleary, Thomas. 2005. The Book of Five Rings.Pg.6. Shambhala Books

(6) Yerkow, Charles. 1942. Modern Judo; The Complete Ju-Jutsu Library. Pp. 20. The Military Service Publishing Co.

(7) Gracie, Renzo. Danaher, John. 2003. Mastering Jujitsu. Pp 12-13.Human Kinetics

(8) Hancock, Irving. 1904. Jiu-Jitsu Combat Tricks Pp. 12-13. Putnam Publishers

(9) Mitchell, David. 1984. Overlook Martial Arts Handbook. Pp. 32. Antler Books. The Overlook Press.

(10) Craig, Darrell. 1995.Japan's Ultimate Martial Art. Pp.3. Tuttle Publishing

(11) Hoare, Syd. 2009. http://www.sydhoare.com/FUSEN.pdf

(12) Masao, Kitami. Clark, Tim. 2007. The Swordless Samurai. Pp.xiv. St.Martin's Press

(13) Nitobe, Inazo. 1969. Bushido; the Soul of Japan. Pp. 67 Charles E. Tuttle Publishing Co.

(14) Morehei, Ueshiba.Stevens, John. 1992. The Art of Peace. Pp. 89. Shambhala Publishing

(15) Tzu, Sun. Cleary, Thomas. 1998. The Art of War. Pg.113. Shambhala Books

JUJITSU OFFICIAL HAIKU

Spring cherry blossoms

Bringing the tiger's eye forth

Giving inner strength

Haiku poems were written by the Samurai and consisted of 17 syllables. The words of the poem also had to indicate what season the 17 syllable poem or Haiku was written in. This indication of the season was referred to as "Kigo". If the poem did not have a reference to the season, it was not recognized as haiku and was called senryu.

HAIKU FORMAT

RULES
1st LINE = 5 Syllables

2nd Line = 7 Syllables

3rd Line = 5 Syllables

FINAL WORD

I hope you enjoyed my book. Now it is your book. Practice is the key to one day becoming a master in anything you are working to become proficient in. If you are as obsessed about martial arts as I am, you will read this book again and again. I feel this book is not the most comprehensive guide ever assembled, and it is most certainly not meant to be. This is the basic guide for the style of Jujitsu.

Knowledge only gives you a mental edge however, it is this mental edge of having more knowledge coupled with the skill in the application of the knowledge that makes you "better".

Sincerely,

Kambiz Mostofizadeh
Author
Mikazuki Jujitsu Manual

MIKAZUKI PUBLISHING HOUSE TITLES

Mikazuki Jujitsu Manual
ISBN-10: 0615473113 (Print)

ISBN-13: 9780615473116 (Print)

ISBN-10: 0615480543 (E-Book)

Pages: 125 (Print)

Release Date: May 2011

Print Retail Price: $24.99

E-book Retail Price: $14.99

Description: Jujitsu was the battlefield art of the Samurai who used the techniques to defend themselves when they had lost their weapon and were facing an armed opponent. But in today's environment where random violence is a certainty, the knowledge of jujitsu has empowered countless individuals with the art of the samurai for self defense. The book by Kambiz Mostofizadeh is a jujitsu manual explaining core jujitsu techniques, shares the principles and applications of ju or yielding, covers Jujitsu's Japanese origins, teaches methods for fighting against multiple attackers, includes techniques for defeating mixed martial artists, and divulges strategies for offensive and defensive maneuvers. The book features more than 20 hand drawn illustrations representing the various techniques used within jujitsu. Mikazuki Jujitsu Manual; Learn Jujitsu also features a glossary of jujitsu terms, annual jujitsu tournaments, and methods for defeating a boxer. The author said "I wrote this book as a guide for my students and any student of modern martial arts. I believe all people can benefit from the study of martial arts, because the need for personal safety and protection is essential to everyone"

Karate 360

ISBN-10: 0983594627 (Print)

ISBN-13: 9780983594628 (Print)

ISBN-13: 978-0-9835946-7-3 (E-book)

Print Retail Price: $14.99

E-book Retail Price: $4.99

Pages: 115 (Print)

Release Date: December 2011

Description: Explore Karate's roots, learn key karate techniques, and learn why Karate is the world's most popular martial art.

EXCERPT - "The essence of Karate is defense. The powerful leg strikes, efficient blocking techniques, and strong punches evolved in to an effective martial art that eventually became the most popular martial art in the world. "

25 Principles of Martial Arts

ISBN-10: 0983594600 (Print)

ISBN-13: 9780983594604 (Print)

ISBN-10: 0983594619 (E-Book)

Pages: 111 (Print)

Release Date: November 2011

Print Retail Price: $14.99

E-book Retail Price: $7.99

EXCERPT - "Large amount of resources and more individuals in your organization do not necessarily equate to victory over your opponent if you have lost the advantage of formlessness."

Letting the Customers Win
ISBN-10: 0983594651 (Print)

ISBN-13: 9780983594659 (Print)

ISBN-13: 978-0-9835946-8-0 (E-book)

Pages: 120

Release Date: February 2011

Print Retail Price: $14.99

E-book Retail Price: $9.99

Description: Millions of dollars are spent to attract customers, while little is spent to keep current customers happy. It is 7 more times expensive to gain new business than it is to keep your current customer. This book reveals customer care strategies including call center management, customer loyalty card schemes, and relationship marketing.

Find the Ideal Husband

ISBN-10: 0983594694 (E-book)

ISBN-13: 9780983594697 (E-book)

Pages: 110 (E-book)

Release Date: Valentine's Day 2012

E-book Retail Price: $9.99

Description: The ideal husband is rich, classy, happy, handsome, and caring. Learn where to meet the ideal husband and how to recognize the indicators for knowing he is the right choice. Let the search begin!

Learning Magic
ISBN-10: 0983594635 (Print)

ISBN-13: 978-0983594635 (Print)

Pages: 111 (Print)

Release Date: March 2012

Print Retail Price: $14.99

Description: Learn the fundamentals of performing magic including the reasons why magic tricks are so effective. Whether at home, in the office, or at a gathering, this book will teach you key magic tricks for performing.

Political Advertising Manual
ISBN-10: 0983594643 (Print)

ISBN-13: 9780983594642 (Print)

ISBN-13: 978-0-9835946-8-0 (E-book)

Pages: 119 (Print)

Release Date: Jan 2012

Print Retail Price: $14.99

E-book Retail Price: $9.99

Description: Political marketing strategies are used by nearly every victorious candidate to achieve electoral victory. Explore key political marketing techniques and effective tactics for effective message delivery.

Other Titles Coming Soon

Visit www.MikazukiPublishingHouse.com for more info

Mikazuki Publishing House is a book publishing company specializing in a variety of non-fiction works.

Press Contacts interested in arranging press interviews and/or author appearances, are welcome to contact:

pr@MikazukiPublishingHouse.com for info

We believe that the written word is the most

effective vehicle for the delivery of knowledge and

that reading is essential to educating oneself.

Mikazuki Publishing House believes in the

promotion of reading as a tool for self

progression and therefore invests resources,

working with libraries and institutions of higher

learning, to propagate the advantages of reading.

Mikazuki Publishing House also offers free book donations and free book signings/appearances to libraries upon request (upon availability).

Mikazuki Publishing House is honored to be an active participant in the fight to reverse world deforestation. Approximately 30 million trees are cut down in the U.S. every year to be used for the creation of print books.

We wish to offset and counterbalance the use of paper in the book publishing industry by working with organizations dedicated to reversing the trend of world deforestation.

We will first start with one tree. The consequences of not doing so could be disastrous for future generations.

Every minute over 160 acres of land feel the destructive effects of deforestation. Deforestation causes species to become extinct, disrupts natural habitats, and erodes the top soil of viable farming lands causing drought and famine.

As a responsible book publisher, Mikazuki Publishing House will donate a percentage from the sale of each book to the effort of planting millions of trees.

Mikazuki Publishing House is pleased to invite foundations, associations, and groups dedicated to planting trees to contact us.

Please send all requests to:
philanthropy@MikazukiPublishingHouse.com

Mikazuki Publishing House is a proud member of the Independent Book Publishers Association (IBPA)

www.ingramcontent.com/pod-product-compliance
Lightning Source LLC
Chambersburg PA
CBHW060940040426
42445CB00011B/946